The Threshing Floor
Broken To Worship

Jeremy J. Brown

© 2017 by Jeremy J. Brown
The Threshing Floor - *Broken To Worship*

Cover design by Harrod Publishing
Editing by Tracy Morgan

Unless otherwise identified, Scripture quotations are from the HOLY BIBLE, NEW INTERNATIONAL VERSION ®, Copyright © 173, 178, 194 by International Bible Society used by permission of Zondervan Publishing House. All rights reserved. Scripture quotations identified KJV are from the King James Version of the Bible.

All rights reserved. No part of this publication may be reproduced, stored in a retrieval system, or transmitted in any form or by any means -- electronic, mechanical, photocopying, recording, or otherwise -- without the prior written permission of the publishers and copyright owners.

Author's Email: pastorjbpfmi@yahoo.com
Publishers Email: harrodenterprises@gmail.com

Published by Harrod Publishing
Clinton, Maryland 20735
www.harrodpublishing.com
home: (301) 828-0331

Printed in the United States Harrod Publishing

THE THRESHING FLOOR — BROKEN TO WORSHIP
JEREMY J. BROWN

ISBN-10: 0-692-85241-7
ISBN-13: 978-0-692-85241-5

Acknowledgements

I must give all glory, adoration and honor to my Lord and Savior, Jesus Christ, for trusting me with His will to go forth into the world and preach the gospel. Without Him, I am nothing.

To the Perfecting Faith Ministries International family who steadily keep me in prayer and hold me accountable for the work of Jesus Christ;

To my lovely wife, Letty; son, Manasseh; and daughter, Jaelyn, who keep me grounded as a husband and father;

To my Apostles Desmond and Lady Forde, for speaking into my life and teaching me the ways of the Lord;

To Bishop Sherlock and Lady Padmore, who charged me to walk worthy of the call;

An enormous thanks to my mother, LaDonna Johnson, for putting up with me at all costs;

And to Robert and LaWanna Harrod, my uncle and aunt; whom the Lord used as markers in my life.

If I have forgotten anyone, please do not hold it against me, for you are in my heart and prayers. Bless you all mightily, in Jesus' name.

Preface

This book is a spiritual study and kingdom purpose–driven text given by the Holy Spirit to encourage, strengthen and enlighten the believers of Jesus Christ. This is to help us open our spiritual eyes and ears, and recognize the Lord's process for each of our lives. It is the voice of His spirit and flows in the true worship, gifting, and offices that are ordained to us before this world existed. It is written in the focus of true worship, but is not limited to true worship, but also what our foundations should be for any ministry the Lord has called us to fulfill.

This book was also written to help us maximize our potential in Jesus, per the plan of our Lord and Savior (Jeremiah 29:11). It is written to help us impact this world, which is lost; and to bring the spirit of revival, true worship, praise, power, repentance, and anointing of the Living God back in our churches for the last day push so that we may be a church accepted without spots or wrinkles. I pray these words will help and enlighten everyone in their walk with Jesus Christ, strengthen their desire and passion for the things of God and finally, that these words will push every reader to their destiny. Amen.

Introduction

I am not, by any measure, a writer or consider myself to be a scholar or scribe. As a matter of fact, I dislike writing of any sort. Perhaps this is why my mother always told me I had "doctor's handwriting" and that my penmanship looked as if a chicken scratched the paper (Thank You, Jesus, for computers!). Even being a degreed belt-holder, a military veteran, and an educated person, I do not consider myself to be a genius who can assemble eloquent words together to move or sway a crowd. So, as I listened to Apostle Desmond Forde preach on a Wednesday night about Gideon pressing wheat in a wine press and heard the voice of the Lord say to me, "It's time to write and release the words I have given you," it brought me to tears. The Lord was saying we must use what He has given us to create in any place we are, and that it will not be accomplished by our flesh, but by His spirit.

The word declares in Judges 6:14 (KJV), *"And the Lord looked upon him, and said, Go in this thy might, and thou shalt save Israel from the hand of the Midianites . . ."*

In other words, God has already supplied to you, in the realm of the spirit, to be able to create, conquer, overtake, press forward and establish His kingdom on earth! The Lord will give you all you need according to the assignment on your life that is securely wrapped up in your God–given destiny.

Chapter 1

Introduction to the Threshing Floor

The threshing floor is a very peculiar and strategic place for the people of God that no one wants to visit or experience. It is not for the faint of heart. The process can be timely and painful but, it is also very necessary. In fact, the actual process is mentioned throughout the Word of God about 26 times with examples found in the story of Gideon threshing wheat in the wine press to Uzzah's death at Nachon's threshing floor, just to name a few. There are many variations, revelations, and books about the threshing floor experience, but this book concerns the revelation the Lord has given me, in the spirit, through my experience with Him.

A wise man once said to me, "You cannot be a tour guide to a country where you have never been." Your experience is priceless and holds more weight than gold and silver. The testimonies and trials of the Lord become testimonies for us, offering insight and wisdom to others. What we have endured is not for us, but for others to be strengthened in the spirit to finish the race.

Let's begin with the introduction of the Prophet Isaiah who served the Lord during the days of Uzziah, Jotham, Ahaz and Hezekiah – the kings of Judah. The Lord allowed me a spiritual look into Isaiah's life and process to bring understanding and wisdom to the people of God.

In sixth chapter of the book of Isaiah, scripture tells us Isaiah was taken up in the Spirit of the Lord and he saw Him high and lifted up. He declared that the angels cried one to another, "Holy, holy, holy is the Lord of hosts: the whole earth is full with His glory." This experience caused him to acknowledge the true glory of God, to experience true worship, and to see who he was and who God is. It also brought Isaiah into the revelation of understanding that he had to be processed by the Spirit of the Lord from where he was, to where he was going. When the Lord shows you the state you are in, you will never truly understand it until you realize where the Lord wants to take you.

Most of the time we truly believe we are saved and serving in the will of God, not knowing that our thoughts and actions are betraying us, causing us to fall further and further away from what Jesus Christ established His church to be. For us to know the will of God, we must know ourselves in Christ, so we must know Him first.

Now, more than ever in today's society, we as a people have become a headstrong, proud, stiff-necked people who have conformed to the world and its way of thinking, acting and functioning. Even our speech, dress and attitudes do not represent or match the kingdom of God anymore.

Now we have numerous church functions, conferences, and workshops portraying that we truly understand what true worship is, what our purpose and calls are, and what is acceptable unto the Lord. We jump through microwave processes instead of going through the real Godly processes.

The Word of God found in Isaiah 1:12-14 (KJV) says,

"When ye come to appear before me, who hath required this at your hand, to tread my courts? Bring no more vain oblations; incense is an abomination unto me; the new moons and sabbaths, the calling of assemblies, I cannot away with; it is iniquity, even the solemn meeting. Your new moons and your appointed feasts my soul hateth: they are a trouble unto me; I am weary to bear them."

Where is the Lord in what we are doing? Where is His glory? His presence? His power? Why are not the words in the Bible physically manifesting right before our very eyes anymore? Where are the true worshippers? Where are the truly called people of God? Where are His people who are called by His name? Where are brokenness and humbleness? We, as a people, need to get back to the threshing floor of God so the Lord may be pleased with His harvest of worship!!

The Lord had to bring Isaiah to His throne room in the spirit to allow him to experience the nature of true worship, humbleness, brokenness, obedience and what His glory was all about. God had to break down Isaiah's flesh and his carnal thinking, and leave him in a broken place so that the true nature of his spirit could not only embrace the presence of God, but so it could also push him to where the Lord wanted him to go for the kingdom.

His visitation with the Lord brought the prophet Isaiah to a place where he was chosen and harvested; shaken and sifted, and humbled and broken. In the end, Isaiah was cleaned up, refreshed and then both sent and marked!

Many people, myself included, have had to go through this process and will continue to go through this process many times over, until the coming of our Lord and Savior Jesus Christ. Philippians 1:6 (KJV) declares:

"Being confident of this very thing, that he which hath begun a good work in you will perform it unit the day of Jesus Christ."

This is an experience Isaiah had to go through many times throughout his lifetime. Because I thought I truly knew the Father and His will for my life while living a partial life relationship with Jesus Christ – operating in the gifting's of God while living in the world – I now realize that although I have gone through this process, I will continue going through these processes.

In these days and times, people do not know the difference between "gift" and "anointing." As the "blind leading the blind," we are all falling into the world's ditches. I have seen it with my own two eyes and have even been a part of it.

Ministering mime/dance with movement and understanding of the ministry pieces or, singing a song entirely with riffs and runs had me thinking I was doing something special. Because people cried or because a praise break followed afterward, not only was I fooled, but so were others. The only one who was not fooled was the Lord our God. Just like the Word says. man looks at the outward appearance; but the Lord our God sees the heart!!

I began singing at the age of seven. I entered the ministry of mime and dance in 2008, and began performing pastoral duties in 2012 until now and beyond. I was even blessed with the wonderful opportunity to minister at the nationally broadcast

Gospel Super Fest with Bishop Hezekiah Walker, and to minister live on an internationally televised program called *Tempo* based out of St. Martin. I have been chauffeured with police escorts, ridden with ambassadors, and have been featured at international conferences, all for which I give God all of the glory.

All of these privileges could not compare to what God was trying to get me to understand in the past. He was trying to get the sin out of my life, and He desired that I allow my true nature, the real me (which is His spirit). To come forth so that His glory could be seen on earth. Yes, your gift will make room for you, but it is the anointing and only the anointing that will break any yoke.

It is not your gift or charisma; not any protocols, degrees, or traditions; not even how long you have been saved, in ministry, or doing whatever it is you believe to be acceptable that breaks yokes. It is not you, me or anyone else: It is the power of God through Jesus Christ that does it! The Lord said it this way: "It is not by power nor by might, but by My Spirit." So, as I, along with many others, have done and am doing, live holy and humble yourselves under the mighty hand of God, and He will exalt you in due time and!!!

I am not preaching, but I *am* being transparent. It seems no one wants to be transparent anymore. People want to hide behind titles and names to cover up their sin. Others never see who you are and what you are doing behind closed doors. Whatever we do in the dark shall surely come to light. I've been there and have done that, living a slack sinful life in the church, thinking my worship or what I called being saved was a sweet-smelling scent in God's nostrils . . . like I was doing God a favor. The

Lord had to expose me to get my attention so that I could repent and be truly delivered . . .

Back in 2008, I was stationed in Mississippi serving in both the military and in ministry. I was arrested and punished for driving under the influence of alcohol. My whole world began crumbling down around me. I had thought I could fool God and those around me, but my prideful, sinful ways caused me to be disgraced and exposed as a supposed child of God. I had been living just like the world, but proclaiming Jesus Christ.

How could I face people now, talking about Jesus Christ?

I thank the Lord for His chastisement, for open rebuke is better than secret love. Indeed, I lost everything: my military career, my wife at the time, money and respect. But what I gained in return was worth the exposure. I gained the greatest thing ever: a true relationship with Jesus Christ.

You cannot live in the world and come into the Lord's presence and believe you are doing the things of God, how He wants you to do them. It is time out for living halfway, teetering on the fence – living anyway we see fit, for your understanding of what is holy and righteous is not God's example. 1 Corinthians 6:9-10 plainly tells us about the kind of life many of the children of God are living. You cannot enter into the kingdom of God with these type of lifestyles choices.

Repent, so that times of refreshing may come from being in the presence of the Lord! "Repent," the Lord speaks from His throne to His Footstool . . . "Repent!" All ye that have an ear, hear what the Spirit of the Lord is saying: "Repent!"

I want to see God's glory rain pour out upon all flesh, as He promised by the mouth of the prophet Joel, for the latter rain to be greater than the former rain!! You must understand: The angels could only worship and operate out of what they saw, experienced and could relate to. Therefore, they all cried "Holy, holy, holy is the Lord of Hosts!!" "Be ye Holy, for I am Holy," says the Lord of Hosts. We must do the same, people of God. Time is of the essence! All ye land, repent and let's get to the threshing floor so we can be broken to worship!

Chapter 2

The Threshing Floor

"Threshing" is the process of loosening the edible part of cereal grain (inner-part) (or soul-spirit) from the scaly, inedible chaff (flesh) that surrounds it. It is the step in grain preparation after harvesting and before winnowing, which separates the loosened chaff from the grain. Threshing may also be done by beating the grain using a flail.

As you can see, this is not a quick microwave process, but a delicate, timely process. At times, it can be a rigorous journey, the race (process) is not given to the swift nor the battle to the strong, but to those who endure (go through) it. In these days, we want the "now" without the process. Let's be honest . . . in today's convenient society, things are being made and delivered at an alarmingly quickened pace, and we have been treating the process of God the same way: "I want what I want, and I want it now!"

Any truly mature Christian would tell you that's not how God operates. His timing and ways are not like ours. It is a process whether we like it or not, whether we want to go through it or not, it is still a process.

Process: A series of actions or steps taken to achieve a particular end. In Hebrew, this word process is *dokime* which means proof of genuineness, approval through testing.

God will always test us our faith, patience, love, or obedience so that we would give Him the glory just as He did in the book of Job. God allowed the enemy to take everything away from him and to even afflict his body. The only thing the enemy could not do was kill Job because he didn't have the power or authority to do so. Job's life was under the protective covering of God.

The various tests and trials we must go through are specifically designed for us and no one else. With bitterness in her heart, Job's wife told him he should curse God and die. You can always determine when the test belongs to you and was not made for another person. The other person will always look on your test sheet (life, problems, and situation) and give you the wrong answers, not knowing their test and your test were on two entirely different subjects.

The test of bodily affliction and the other things Job was made to endure were made for him, not his wife. Her test was to determine if she would strengthen and back her husband in the Lord through this process. She failed miserably. The process is the test, and the test is the process to find out if you are worthy of the calling, for we are all called to be saints and to worship.

Okay, let's look at this process from God's perspective. As I said, the Prophet Isaiah had to be first called/chosen by God. When the Master Farmer (God) is set to select a crop to be grown, He must choose the right seed to place in the ground at the right time, and in the right season. Seeds and plants cannot grow in just any season; the season must be perfect. Some seasons call for rain, some for drought, and others call for coolness.

You cannot plant rice in a season you would plant wheat; you must plant in the perfect season for rice. Ecclesiastes declares:

"To everything, there is a season and a time to every purpose under heaven."

Not only must the atmosphere, which is the right season (God's Will/Presence), exist, but the ground must be fertile, tilled and ready. This is where the kingdom is experiencing a great problem.

For some strange reason, we are trying to skip the right season and expect excellent results; but all of those things – seasons, atmosphere, and the ground (Father, Son and the Holy Spirit) must come together in unity for all of them to work. The word declared: "let us make man in our image and likeness." Let us plant of our spirit to reap a bountiful harvest of supernatural results!

In John 15, Jesus told us, "I am the true vine and my Father is the husbandman." In some translations, this term "husbandman" means **land worker and or farmer**, displaying the nature of God as The Master Farmer in the sense that He plants, waters, watches and then harvests what is good to Him.

Now look at it this way: if God wants to grow apples, He will place an apple seed, at the right time, into fertile ground and water it. The seed He plants is a pure seed of His spirit and not a hybrid (I will touch on this hybrid part later), but pure, holy and righteous, and He expects to get something out of it in return.

What God plants must not only grow, but also produce fruit and seed (Genesis 1:11-12)!

The Lord expects so much more from us in this life. He has given us what we need to make sure we are giving back to the Lord what is due to Him: our worship and our lives!

Chapter 3

The Chosen Harvest

I liken the seed to the call the Lord has upon your life and ministry, and how He wants it to operate here on this earth. But remember, the Lord chooses what call, path, anointing and/or office He has ordained and chosen for your life.

Many people jump into offices, lifestyles, callings and anointing God has not appointed for their lives. For example, you contend, "I'm an apple," but instead, you come out looking and tasting like a sour prune. Something is wrong. We represent ourselves, at times, as the fig tree that deceived Jesus. The deceitful fig tree said it was ready to give fruit by the appearance of its leaves, but in reality, it was fruitless and barren. Now we, like the fig tree, have the appearance of being chosen and possessing titles and even degrees, but we are fruitless and barren, having no fruit (God's anointing) to give.

The Bible tells us that when Jesus saw this deception, He cursed the tree. Because Jesus rejected it, the earth also rejected it. This is actually how the disciples could see the roots. Let's back this up with scripture: Ephesians 4:11-12 tells us . . .

"He gave some, apostles; and some, prophets; and some evangelists; and some, pastors and teachers; For the perfecting of the saints, for the work of the ministry, for the edifying of the body of Christ:"

Not everyone who wants to be a part of a dance/mime/worship team or desires a leadership position in ministry is called to do so or to operate as such. This is why the Word declares that many are called, but few are chosen. The spirit of the Lord must call and choose you! If and only if He has called and chosen you, will the Lord back you with His anointing!

In the Word of God,1 Sam 8-13, Saul stepped out of his royal anointing to operate as a priest and offer up burnt sacrifices, but God did not receive either his sacrifice or his worship. Understand, if we are working in a calling, lifestyle, office or anointing that has not been given to us by the Lord God Almighty, Himself, The Lord will not receive what we are giving. He will reject it just as he rejected Saul's worship and the deceitful fig tree.

In addition to having callings and anointings upon our lives, we are also soldiers in the Lord's Army. We are built and armored for war! If we were not, then the Apostle Paul would have never commanded us to put on the whole armor of God in the book of Ephesians. Certain calls, graces, anointings, offices, mantles, and lifestyles have armor that is directly fitted and tailor-made to the person's spirit and for the kingdom task upon them. With that said, when the enemy comes to shoot his fiery darts at us while we are wearing the wrong armor for our kingdom tasks (calls, graces, anointing, offices, mantles, and lifestyles), they will afflict and wound us considerably because the armor we are wearing is not tailor-made for our assignment or call. This is why David couldn't wear the armor belonging to Saul. It didn't fit for the task of not only protecting him, but killing the uncircumcised Philistine, Goliath.

Everything David needed had already been given to him, in the spirit, by the Lord our God. All I am asking of you, children of God, is to allow His Spirit to call you into the ministry that He wants for you, and He will anoint you for the task ahead. God will back you, and He will use you for His honor and glory (1 Samuel 17:38-51, Ephesians 6:10-17).

Ministry, whether it is pastoral; prophetic; dance; mime, or worship (or any part of ministry the Lord has called you to) is not for the pleasing of man, to gain riches or wealth, or to be famous.

Ministry is to allow God to use you as He sees fits and to bless Him, first, with the gifting's and talents He has given you. Then, it is to bless His people and to edify them spiritually by His spirit, but also to destroy the kingdom of darkness and its works. It is a spiritual battle, people of God, so we need to know who we are and who and what we are fighting. We cannot be deceived or, as Apostle Paul mentioned, be ignorant of the enemy's devices.

First, God is not coming down to do anything. He has done everything, in the spirit, already. God chooses and calls us to be used to manifest His glory on earth. He has ordained us as His children to have dominion over and in this earthly realm. Could you imagine if God allowed us to pick what we wanted to do in His kingdom? If He did, then He truly would not be God. Instead, He would be a magic genie who grants your every wish and command. Every time you would rub the golden lamp, He would pop out. Thank God He, the Lord, our God, is sovereign, and can do *what* He wants, *when* He wants, *how* He wants, and can even *choose* as He wants!

As the Lord chooses, plants, and waters in the correct season – when the crop is ripe; the Lord will also harvest His crop, but this is just the beginning of our threshing floor process. Just because the Lord has called you, you will never and I repeat, NEVER, ever have arrived. We must remember to stay on the potter's table. The Lord told me that some of His people are trying to access the glory of the Lord without going through the process He has set before them.

Look at the life of Elisha in 1 Kings 19. We see that the Lord had chosen Elisha to be the prophet in succession to Elijah, while Elijah had hidden in the cave from the threats of Jezebel. Know that Jezebel will always come up against the process and potential of a true child of God. That wicked, demonic Jezebel spirit wants nothing more than to kill, steal from and destroy any saint in the kingdom of God.

Understand this: the spirit of Jezebel is highly prevalent and crafty. It is operating in many of our churches and people to throw them off course from the greater glory that is going to be revealed in these last days. This demon not only hates and fights against the true prophetic, but also against the divine order of God. In this function, this same demon was trying to stop Elisha from being harvested because he was already chosen.

Just because you are saved doesn't mean that it will always be clear sailing and blue waters on your narrow road to be where the Lord wants and needs you to be. There will be many obstacles along the way, both great and small, but these obstacles are only tests and training grounds for where you are going in the Lord. So, stay in the process! Faith that has not been tested cannot be trusted. The Word of the Lord declares that God gives each man a measure of faith. Your God-given measure is tested against the storms of life that come your way, just to see if your faith and obedience is foundationally grounded in Jesus Christ. The Lord just wants to see how much you will move – or not move – from the rock when the heavy winds and rains of life come your way. If you can withstand one storm, it will build your faith for the next one.

Chapter 4

Harvested

In the book of 1 Kings, the 19th chapter and the 19th we learn of the very first encounter Elijah had with Elisha. Elisha was being harvested (pulled or uprooted from where he was to where he was going in Christ) and meeting Elijah was the next step in his threshing floor process. It is almost funny to me how Elisha was tilling the grown with oxen, preparing to plant seed for a harvest and unbeknownst to him, he was about to be harvested out of the place he was. You see, when Elijah passed by Elisha who was plowing with the oxen, the Bible tells us that Elijah cast his mantle upon Elisha and Elisha ran after him, leaving the oxen and his family behind, and he followed the man of God.

Elijah's mantle was like a spiritual sickle, cutting away Elisha's earthly roots and ties with his family, home, lifestyle and place of comfort. Being harvested, in this sense. is going to pull you away from a place where you are grounded, comfortable and complacent. When I was called, chosen and harvested for the ministry of mime and dance back in 2008 and then again in 2012 for the pastoral call that was upon my life; this is exactly what happened to me. Therefore, in my harvesting experience, I was taken totally out of my comfort zone and place. I knew nothing about this type of ministry and beyond that; I couldn't even dance or preach. Yes, I know . . . very funny, right?

In 2012, I was enjoying a time of prayer and fasting with the Lord while sitting in my house in Curacao, when the Lord spoke to me. He told me that my Apostle, who at that time was just my friend and brother in Christ, was coming and that I was being shifted into the pastoral call and to submit to the plan He had put on my Apostle's heart for ministry. I knew the Prophetic call was already upon me, but this was a heavyweight – a mega bomb – the Holy Spirit had just dropped on me. I was very comfortable with my life, not being seen, singing a song or two with the praise team, going out to minister in mime, and sitting in the back attending what we call "church."

The questions and concerns, and the fear of messing things up for God hit me all at once. I am the type of person who thinks very deeply about the care of others, and my mode of thinking was: *"If I mess up, I not only abort my future, but I hurt others in the process, for what comes from the head goes down to the body."* But even with all the doubts and concerns I had, my spirit still said "Yes," as my Apostle spoke to me that day about what the Lord had told him and the directions he was given to start Perfecting Faith Ministries International.

My Apostle laid the mantle that was given to him by the Holy Spirit on me with the laying of hands and I received what the Lord ordained for me through the spirit. All of the cares, concerns and doubts I had disappeared. I left everything behind that day just to pick up my cross and follow Jesus on the way to this new chapter and book in my life – for His glory and honor!! Amen!!

Now . . . before I totally surrendered, I was still living in the world, going to clubs; drinking; partying; fornicating; listening to worldly music; . . . you name it, I was doing it. I was still acting like a Christian on certain days, or on just those days when I put myself into a situation I couldn't get myself out of. Sounds a little familiar perhaps? Maybe? If this is you, please, and I say *"please,"* quickly repent and turn from your wicked ways. Time is running out!

Having been chosen for a ministry does not mean you are perfect, and you should never use your selection as an excuse to sin; but the Lord takes imperfect people to impact imperfect people. The good work the Lord has started in us, He will perform until the coming of His Son, Jesus Christ.

The Lord took an "on–the–fence, lukewarm Christian," who really only knew *about* God and not of His ways, and chose him before he was even in his mother's womb just as Jeremiah 1:5 states. He was picked out and set aside. Then, God pulled me unto Himself and continued with my threshing floor process. Whew! Even though I am a Southeast Washington D.C. native – "Hail to the Redskins!" – now living on the beautiful island of Curacao with my wonderful wife, Letty; my son, Manasseh (Junior); and my daughter Jaelyn (Jelly), and having adapted to Caribbean island life, I feel a good ole American praise break on that!

As I said before, I can only speak from the experience that the Lord has allowed me to go through by His grace and mercy!! Make sure that you never take what we don't even deserve for granted any longer. If the Lord has plucked you after being chosen, He has done it for an incredible reason! The Lord revealed to my spirit why a plant, fruit, or what has been planted at the perfect (mature) time must be harvested. The Lord said to me, *"If you leave it in the place where it was planted and miss the time of harvest when it is ripe and ready, whatever was planted will stay there to decompose and die."* So, tell the Lord "Thank You!" for pulling you out of your comfort zone (dead place) and throwing you into your future!

Chapter 5

The Shaking/Sifting/Separation

I heard a song by Jekalyn Carr entitled "Greater Is Coming." Some of the lyrics are:

"I feel a shaking in the spirit, I feel a beating in the spirit, I feel a pressing in the spirit."

This is one of the most pivotal and important aspects, in my opinion. that has to take place – the being shaken. In Hebrews 12:25-29 (MSG), it reads:

"So don't turn a deaf ear to these gracious words. If those who ignored earthly warnings didn't get away with it, what will happen to us if we turn our backs on heavenly warnings? His voice that time shook the earth to its foundations; this time—he's told us this quite plainly—he'll also rock the heavens: 'One last shaking, from top to bottom, stem to stern.' The phrase 'one last shaking' means a thorough housecleaning, getting rid of all the historical and religious junk so that the unshakable essentials stand clear and uncluttered.

Do you see what we've got? An unshakable kingdom! And do you see how thankful we must be? Not only thankful, but brimming with worship, deeply reverent before God. For God is not an indifferent bystander. He's actively cleaning house, torching all that needs to burn, and he won't quit until it's all cleansed. God himself is Fire!"

Let's break this down to get a better understanding:

In this context, when the Apostle Paul talks of God's voice shaking the earth, it speaks of our flesh, carnal thinking, earthly ways, evil foundations and wicked thoughts. God made a man out of the earth and breathed the breath of life into him, and he became a living soul. Now the breath of life, which in the Greek is "nshamah," means "the wind or vital breath," and one of my favorite definitions, "divine inspiration, intellect."

Something, God's spirit, must be released into the earthen outer shell of a man to get to the core of his soul and to start shaking himself out of himself. Tell the Lord, "Breath in me again and again so I can be filled with something greater than myself; something greater than my ways, my thinking and my intellect!"

It violently shakes and breaks off what you thought you knew about God, yourself, and the course or path you are walking and operating in. This is why the visitation in the realm of the spirit in Isaiah 6 shook the prophet so badly. What Isaiah thought he knew about God, the realm of the spirit and worship was totally destroyed; but what the prophet took in through his spiritual eyes, downloaded into his spirit and began to make a foundational change in his mindset. It made him shake off his high-mindedness concerning living what he thought was a life pleasing unto the Lord. The Bible encourages us in 2 Corinthians 10:5 (KJV):

"Casting down imaginations, and every high thing that exalteth itself against the knowledge of God, and bringing into captivity every thought to the obedience of Christ."

We must allow the ingested Word and Spirit of God to shake these thoughts and imaginations out of us, so we can be in Christ with the mind of Christ. Paul commanded us to "Let this mind be in you as it also was in Christ Jesus!" If our thoughts are not of the Spirit of the Lord, they will betray us and we will become modern-day Sadducees and Pharisees . . . being very religious, but not having any relationship.

Like the Sadducees and the Pharisees, we know it all. Nobody can tell us anything (rebuke) because either we are aware of the law, or because we have been in ministry for such a long time we just simply know everything – no one can teach us anything; you cannot judge me. Well if that's the case and you are unteachable, then you are God on earth (vicar) and should convert to being Catholic so you can become a pope. High-mindedness will not get us to God; our obedience will. Those mindsets are nothing but pure pride. Our God said that He even hates a proud look.

This mid-point in the process is not easy, by far. We have things we have practiced for years – religious things, wrong ways, faulty thinking, you name it! Amid it all, God is continuing to work in and on us if we allow Him to and if we stay right there during the process. Don't jump out of the fire; stay there and endure like a good soldier, for the best is yet to come! Remember, the race is not to the swift nor the battle to the strong, but to those who endure!

Now this part of the shaken process, to me, is imperative!! In Hebrews 12, where we left off, the Word spoke of God's voice not only shaking earth, but shaking heaven also. From an aspect of the revelation the spirit of the Lord has given me, He begins with shaking off our fleshy, carnal, earthly ways and thoughts; and then He shakes our spirits and those things attached to our spirit and soul that shouldn't be. Simply put, as someone who is being used as a vessel for deliverance and someone who is also going through it myself, I know how important the shaking is.

As a child of God, we all must go through this part of the process. Most people in the body of Christ don't even believe it's possible that evil, familiar spirits either possess them or are attached to them. This is one of the greatest reasons why men and women of God, in all aspects of ministry and life, are destroyed: the enemy's works, in the realm of the spirit, are attached to or exist in their lives. Many people try to skip this part of the process because of how they will be viewed or what people may say about what took place during their deliverance.

If you fall to the ground, so what! If you throw up, so what! If the demon begins to manifest, so what! We should never be afraid of deliverance – at all. We need to be freed from every spirit that is not of God. From the spiritual wife and husband to the spirit of anger, we, as ministers of the Gospel, have to be shaken and freed by our Lord and Savior, Jesus Christ!!

You must understand where you are coming from, and understand the spiritual, open doors that cause us to be chained and bound by the evil one. Maybe if I had been taught this early on in my life and had understood it, I would not have gotten the DUI charge. Maybe I would not have had to endure all of the bad choices I made; not knowing what was attached to me.

The enemy does not care how old or young you are; how pretty or ugly you might be; how much money you have or what kind of car you drive. His only job is to kill, steal and destroy.

Every believer, Christian, and follower of Jesus Christ must go through deliverance. What you sow (this includes your bloodline), you will reap. The enemy is always looking for ways in and sin allows the doors to our spirit to open and for an unclean spirit to enter. Matt 12:43-45 talks about when unclean spirits leave, but how do they enter? What doors did we open in our lives for sin? What doors did my family and my generations open? What evil covenants have been made by my ancestors and myself? We must all be free from every unclean spirit, whether it is homosexuality, pride, bitterness, malice, stealing, lying, etc.

We must also **want** these unclean spirits to be released or shaken from us. An unclean spirit will not stay where it is not wanted, just like the Holy Spirit will not remain where He is not wanted. That is why we cannot grieve His Holy Spirit. Do you know that your body is the temple of the Holy Spirit?! Understand, this part of the threshing floor process is key to your shaking/deliverance.

David asked the Lord to create in him a clean heart and to renew a right spirit within him – not just any spirit, but a *right* one, a holy and righteous spirit. Following this request, David cried out, asking God not to take His Holy Spirit from him!!! We need to get back to that place on the threshing floor where we repent, and where we are sifted, released, shaken and freed!!

When Isaiah realized what his spiritual faults were and that the things that were attached to him were not of God, he cried out to Him and declared that he, himself was a man of unclean lips:

"There's something on the inside of me that is not of You, and I don't want or need it anymore! Please have mercy on me and deliver me!"

It is something you must want. The Lord will not force anything on you, not anything.

The prophet Isaiah allowed himself to be sifted by the spirit of the Lord. If you look at the word "sift," it means to "put a fine, loose, or powdery substance through a sieve so as to remove lumps or large particles." The other part of the definition I like is "to examine (something) thoroughly so as to isolate that which is most important or useful."

When you look at the sifting tool, it is a large circular, woven pan with a mesh-like substance used to catch what is not needed, which is thrown out, and allows or isolates what is most useful or relevant to pass through and fall to the holy ground. The Lord spoke to me and told me that His shifting tool is His Spirit, which is His will, and when we are placed into this device, only our redeemed spirit/soul can pass through. Those things that are not of God; flesh, impure thoughts, nasty habits, chains of addiction, familiar spirits, etc., none of those things can pass through the thin, fine mesh of His will. We ourselves must enter in *" . . . at the straight gate: for wide is the gate . . . that leadeth to destruction, and many there be which go in thereat: Because strait is the gate, and narrow is the way, which leadeth unto life and few there be that find it."* Matthew 7:13-14 (KJV).

The enemy has blinded the churches, its leaders and its followers by deceiving them into believing this part of the threshing floor process (sifting/shaking/deliverance)is not vital to the success of God's people. Just because you have been ordained by man and have certificates and diplomas, doesn't mean you have been ordained or delivered by God. You can speak in tongues, sing, pay tithes and offering, and still need deliverance. Whatever the Lord has created, the enemy – because he is the "father of lies" – tries his best to pervert and poison it, creating an illusion. In Isaiah 14:12-14, we see the reason why Satan perverts what is holy and righteous, and why he tries to chain you to himself: It was in his heart to be exalted above our true God and to be like the most High.

We need the power of the Almighty one, in Jesus' name, to set us free from every type of wicked bondage! In these last days, doctrines of demons, false teachings and kingdom dividedness are at an all-time high!! Wake up people of God! Be sober and vigilant, knowing that the enemy is like a roaring lion seeking whom he may devour.

The Hebrew for deliverance, (tshuw`ah), is noted for meaning "deliverance, help, safety, salvation, and finally, victory". Psalm 34:19 (KJV) affirms that:

"Many are the afflictions of the righteous: but the Lord delivereth him out of them all."

Freedom from the hands and works of the enemy is Victory! Let no man deceive you, people of God, get delivered! I truly want those of us who are in the kingdom of God to be effective in this walk with Jesus Christ, but first, we must know the truth: Jesus loves us and wants us to be free!

Behind every situation in your life is a demon (unclean spirit). Anything that has the intention or design to kill, steal or destroy your life is not from the Lord, our God. We wrestle not against flesh and blood, but against principalities, powers, the rulers of the darkness of this world, against spiritual wickedness in high places. The Lord Jesus Christ is able and willing to deliver you with His power and anointing . . . if you let Him!!

If you are bound by these familiar, unclean spirits, no matter what it is, I pray the Lord sends an anointed man or woman of God your way, or that you cry out to Jesus and ask Him, just as David did, to create in you a clean heart and to renew a right spirit within you. I also pray that the same fire contained in the coal that was placed on Isaiah's mouth, which was the fire from heaven, consume every demonic spirit and force that is either attached to or afflicting your life in the mighty name of Jesus!! Amen!!

Chapter 6

Humbled and Broken

"Humbled and broken." These two statements and attitudes go together, hand–in–hand, almost like peanut butter and jelly, or the Father, Son and Holy Spirit. They are connected and can't function without each other – a match made in Heaven. You must be humble to be broken; and to be broken, you must be humble. God will not reject a broken heart and a contrite spirit.

Jeremiah 18:1-12 discusses the potter's wheel and refers to what then, and now, is the body of Christ. Verse six asks the question, *". . . Can I not do with you, Israel, as this potter does?"* Our God never and I will say this again, He will **never** force Himself or His process on anyone who doesn't want it, for God so loved the world that He gave His only begotten Son, that whosoever believeth in Him should not perish, but have eternal life. The Lord gave so that we can choose. Wherever it says "should not," we have a choice. God gave men the free will to choose, hence the portion of scripture that admonishes us to *". . . choose you this day whom ye will serve . . .!"*

As a child of God, you must be humble enough to be placed on the potter's wheel. This means you must choose to not only be on the wheel, but to remain on the wheel and allow the brokenness to happen; permit the Master's mighty hands to work in your life. To move past just calling Jesus our Savior to making Him our Lord Jesus Christ, we must be both humble and broken. Jesus Christ earned the title of both Savior and Lord. He gave Himself as a sacrifice – an act He did not have to allow, but did it anyway – just for where we are now, where we came from, and for where we are going in Christ Jesus. God orders the steps of a righteous man, but don't just quote the Scripture – follow it up with acts of obedience. Do not just be a hearer of the Word; act upon it!

The Apostle Paul described himself as "a prisoner wrapped in chains." Ephesians 6:19-20

"Pray also for me, that whenever I open my mouth, divine utterance may be given me, so that I will boldly make known the mystery of the gospel, for which I am an ambassador in chains. Pray that I may proclaim it fearlessly, as I should."

Like Paul, we are also prisoners, realizing we can only do, go, think, and function as the warden (God) has instructed and or allowed. The problem with this part of the threshing floor is that it is very painful. The Lord sees where the cracks are in our lives, the unperfected lines in our spirit and soul that do not reflect His Holy Spirit. He asks us, with our permission, to place ourselves on the potter's wheel. How can this be . . . that we have to give Him permission to do so?

When we pray the Lord's Prayer as we are instructed to, unlike the Sadducees and Pharisees, we speak from our hearts as we declare, *"Let the Thy Kingdom come and Thy will be done on earth as it is in Heaven."* The earth that we talk about is us. God formed these earthly vessels from the dirt and filled us with His Spirit which is life.

God, being the outright owner of everything that is and was made and without Him, nothing was made, can process us at any time in our lives according to His perfect will. As the Lord sees fit, He observes our lives and notes the imperfections that others, and many times we, ourselves, don't see. King David did not see anything wrong with killing his faithful servant Uriah for the opportunity of a lustful and adulterous time with his wife. It was not until the voice of the Lord harkened unto Nathan the Prophet by the telling of a parable, that David became aware of his wicked acts (cracks, imperfections).

We must get back on the wheel, but we must want to *be* and *stay* there. The little cracks can be eased out with less work, but the deep cracks in our lives take a little more effort and work to get rid of . . . fire will accomplish this!!

The deeper the crack in our personality, spirit, thinking, emotions, mind, and soul is, the hotter the fire the Lord will apply to us. While we are on the potter's wheel, the Lord applies the hottest of fires so He can remove the things that are not of Him. Look at it like this: Consider the iron you use to press your clothes. There are many different settings on that iron, but you must select the setting that will work best with the kind of fabric that needs to be pressed.

The setting will dictate the temperature that has to be applied to the material. You cannot use the "linen" setting for a delicate fabric. The Maker of the fabric of man knows exactly what heat to apply to us to press the imperfections out of our lives. His thought and His ways are so much higher than ours, and we must trust in His infinite wisdom. He knows what He is doing! Even when it doesn't feel good, and we don't know what is going on, I will lift up my eyes unto the hills from whence cometh my help. God, He is my rock and my salvation; in Him I will trust.

Moses asked the Lord to teach him His ways, not just His acts . . . but also, His ways! If we know His ways, we will understand *why* the Lord is doing what He is doing and not focus on *what* He is doing. Through all of this, we must still give thanks. The Word declares as we fall into divers temptation, it is for the testing of our patience in faith. You see, the Lord is after our trust in Him. Some men trust in horses and chariots, but I place my confidence in the Lord!!

Chapter 7

Cleaned Up/Refreshed

I combined these two terms because they go hand–in–hand with each other. As I have stated before, you cannot have one without the other. As we look at the harvesting of fruits and vegetables, we know that before any farmer brings his product or produce to the marketplace, he takes a very important last step before exposing his best work, or before displaying his trophy in the market. He washes off the residue that might or could have been left during the threshing floor process.

The woman at the well, as mentioned in John 4, is an example of being cleaned up and refreshed. When the Lord is preparing any us, working on us through His Word, He urges our spirits to come and drink from His well – a well that will never run dry.

The threshing floor process takes such a toll on our emotions, bodies, souls and spirits. This is why we need a fresh drink from the Spirit of God, to revive us for the next push in our lives. As water is to our natural bodies, diluting and cleansing our kidneys and liver of the toxic things we have taken in, so it is with the Spirit of God. As we meditate on the Word day and night, we are being washed and cleansed from the things of this world that poison us. The Message version of 2 Timothy 2:14-18 reads:

"Repeat these basic essentials over and over to God's people. Warn them before God against pious nitpicking, which chips away at the faith. It just wears everyone out. Concentrate on

doing your best for God, work you will not be ashamed of, laying out the truth plain and simple. Stay clear of pious talk that is only talk. Words are not mere words, you know. If they are not backed by a godly life, they accumulate as poison in the soul. Hymenaeus and Philetus are examples, throwing believers off stride and missing the truth by a mile by saying the resurrection is over and done with."

We are commanded to show ourselves approved by God, workers who are not ashamed because we rightly divide the word of truth. In the Spirit, this is our drinking or taking in of His Word. WE have to allow the Word to process through and prepare us while our spiritual kidneys and liver extract and cleanse us from what is not needed as they labor to retain the nutrients that are needed to help our spirits function properly.

As we rid ourselves from the junk of worldly music, movies, conversations, dressings, etc., the Word of God refreshes us. It is, to us, like a cold drink of water on a hot day. I fully understand, now, why the Lord tells us to be either hot or cold. If we are lukewarm, He will spit us out of His mouth.

In spite of my short stature, I have always been an athlete. The Lord has blessed me with athletic gifts ranging from football to wrestling. I can do it all, and very well!

I would play football all day, even on the hottest of days! We would take breaks or timeouts to be refreshed so that we could continue the football game against whomever we were playing at the time. When you need a fresh drink of cold water on an unusually hot day after sweating so much, to be given something lukewarm or hot to drink would cause you to spit it out quickly.

As an athlete, if I did not receive something to refresh and revive me, I would cramp up. Cramping takes place when your muscles fight against you because they have not been hydrated and nourished correctly. It is the same with our spirits. As the world dehydrates us by trying to dry up the anointing on and in our lives, we need a fresh drink so that our spirit man does not cramp up and fight against us. We need Jesus, and we need the Word of God!

As we sit in our assemblies, churches, or even when we read the Word of God on our own, without fail, the Lord will give us just what we need to get us to the next step in our lives –whatever that may be. He gives us that "something" that hits our spirits directly and deals with our spirit, yes I said "spirit," and not our emotions. He gives us that "something" according to the situation we are facing or have just gone through. Allow the word to renew, refresh or rehydrate your spirit, soul, and mind; and do not allow that situation, circumstance, problem, test or trial to lead you to conform to the world and its standards. Do not give up. Press! Press toward the mark for the prize of the high calling in Jesus Christ!

Chapter 8

Sent/Marked

When we look back at Isaiah 6:8-9, we see an excellent example of the conversation between God and the Prophet Isaiah:

"Then I heard the voice of the Lord saying, 'Whom shall I send? And who will go for us?' And I said, 'Here am I. Send me!' He said, 'Go and tell this people: 'Be ever hearing, but never understanding; be ever seeing, but never perceiving.'"

Yes, the Lord has taken us through a very rigorous and lengthy process. In fact, if the Lord had shared exactly how He was going to prepare us, we would have responded: "No give it to someone else." The Lord asked a very simple question of the Prophet Isaiah: "Whom shall I send and who will go for us?" Now this questions bothers me a bit, but it also brings clarity and revelation to the *why* and not the *how*.

Picture yourself standing in the presence of God. He, the Father, has just figuratively taken you through hell and back (Psalm 23); walked through the valley of the shadow of death; and has broken, battered, shattered, and shaken you. He allowed you to be in the fiery furnace just like the three Hebrew boys and you are *yet* standing in Christ Jesus; but the Lord still has a question on His lips: *"Whom shall we send?* Yes, I am laughing about this part.

I am in awe God and of the timing of this question. In response to His question, I asked (to myself, of course), "God, didn't You see what You just put me through, and You still ask me that type of question?" I almost did not make it through the process, seeing how rough it was for me. At this moment, I feel like Sarah and I just want to laugh. Look, I know the God we serve has a sense of humor just as I do. I am sure He is going to make us laugh here and there, just to get a good laugh, Himself. Laughter is such a great medicine, even as the word of God declares.

The question our Lord posed has a very significant meaning. Think about any product that is distributed by a company. As raw material, it goes through a series of processes before it is sent out into the marketplace and reaches the hands of a consumer. One of those processes, the final process, is inspection. Before it actually ends up in the hands of a consumer, it is inspected so that it can be marked by the brand or brand maker. Regarding the spirit, this inspection is to ensure that you are fully capable of carrying the anointing and Spirit of the Lord to the marketplace with His seal.

This seal is vital for where you are going; but it is also task essential, task needy and task orientated. If we look at the life of Jesus right before he was sent to perform miracles, the Word of God tells us that he found John the Baptist preaching in the wilderness and baptizing whomever would come unto him, for the kingdom of God was nigh. Jesus showed up at the baptism asking to be baptized just as any normal person would.

John, serving in the position of a servant/leader and of one who was about to be baptized, did not allow his mental capacity to wrap around the concept of Jesus Christ. The Son of God, who was fully God and fully man and of whom many of the prophets spoke of to come, stood in front of him. The promises of God asked to be baptized by this man who thought of himself as a mere mortal.

This is the inspection component of the threshing floor process. Before you are sent, marked, or just simply commissioned, there must be another "yes" that comes from your heart and spirit unto the Father. But this humble "yes" comes from both understanding and knowing that what you have gone through is not for the now, but for the latter.

Jesus' "yes" was found in His act of submission to the baptism. The Lord will not send you unless this inspection, this "yes," this marking has taken place. The Bible confirms that after Jesus was submerged in the water, the Spirit of the Lord came upon Him like that of a dove. This was the branding/marking of our Lord and Savior Jesus Christ. Without this branding, we would have never heard of all the wonderful signs, miracle and wonders that followed Him. Take notice that all of these wonderful signs, wonders and miracles; and the seal of approval were accomplished after the inspection, and not before.

Do you now understand why it was so important for God to try the Prophet Isaiah again, to see where his mind and heart were concerning where He was taking Isaiah? Because of the "why factor" of our thinking, a lot of people would have taken offense to the question the Lord asked without actually understanding *what* the Lord was asking and *why* He was asking it. If your mind is double-minded, you will be unstable in all your ways and will destroy yourself, your ministry and others.

Some people do not make it through this last phase of the threshing floor because of what's truly in their hearts and minds. The heart is desperately wicked, and who would know but our God? I once heard a very wise and anointed man of God tell me that you must pass every course in the Kingdom of God University. We cannot skip, or move on to the next class or course until we have passed the test that is before us.

God does not and I repeat, ***does not*** grade on a curve. If He did, then when the Lord spoke to the Prophet Amos about the plumb line concerning Israel, He would lied and compromised, possessing no standard or foundation regarding His word. We all know that is not our God. Our God cannot lie and He places His word above His name. He is also no respecter of persons. As far as God is concerned, we are all in the same standard of classes and courses, but those classes and courses are based upon individual criteria focus and the job or assignment God has placed on our lives.

Please review a few points from this portion of the book. I pray they bless you and drive you to dig deeper into the things of the Lord:

1. A marked/sent/inspected approved man or woman of God, should always display their light.
2. A marked/sent/inspected approved man or woman of God should represent whoever has marked them with the seal and sent them.
3. A marked/sent/inspected approved man or woman of God must be content in who they are in Christ.

4. A marked/sent/inspected approved man or woman of God must understand that approval comes from being obedient to the Spirit of God.
5. A marked/sent/inspected approved man or woman of God must understand the rules and regulations for carrying the seal or mark of Jesus Christ.
6. A marked/sent/inspected approved man or woman of God must be and stay humble and not move before the seal is upon them. They must remain humble during and after the sealing process.
7. A marked/sent/inspected approved man or woman of God must understand that they will go through this process many times over a lifetime (from faith to faith, and from glory to glory).
8. Finally, a marked/sent/inspected approved man or woman of God must understand that this is not their end; it is just the beginning.

Chapter 9

Broken To Worship

This is what the Lord had been doing to me throughout the entire threshing floor process: He was taking me through and producing a true worshiper. What happened to our worship, love, and adoration for God and the things of the Kingdom?

It seems like the people of God have been shifted into the love of money, gifts, material things, titles, worshipping man, and selfish thinking. We worship and love the gifts instead of adoring the Giver of the gifts. Do not get me wrong, all of these things are nice, but when they take the place of God, we are playing with Fire. God . . . He is a consuming Fire!

Some of today's preaching and lifestyle choices are pushing people away from Jesus Christ and toward a hybrid form of Christ – not the Christ which is Jesus. We have adopted a form of Godliness, but we deny the power thereof. Not to beat up on anyone, but we must realize this leading away from the true Jesus Christ is the work of Satan and his demons. What I speak is the truth by the spirit of the Lord. If the truth is accepted, it shall make us free.

Worship . . . what is it, truly? How does it apply to my life, mime, dance or ministry? No matter what title, gifting, or anointing we possess, or how the Lord determines to use us, it is essential that worship is first in our lives.

The Lord truly used His infinite wisdom and knowledge to break me and to unmask my true worship of Him, whether it was singing, dancing, miming or my life choices. We must have a lifestyle of worship that is pleasing to our God. The word "worship" means "to reverence, to adore, or to prostrate one's self before that which is greater." On the contrary, we often believe that how good we dance or how we can slay a song is an example of true worship and most of the time; it is not.

Worship has a character that must reflect God's character if it is to be accepted or accessed by His spirit. First and foremost, the most important thing, and please listen very carefully, is that you must have a relationship with the true and living God if you are going to worship Him. Understand, the world cannot worship the King of Kings and the Lords of Lords. You must be a citizen of the Kingdom and be connected by His Spirit in order to truly worship God.

David declared in Psalm 22:3 (KJV):

"But thou art holy, O thou that inhabitest the praises of Israel."

As a prophetic worshipper, I believe David was aware that he tapped into something divine with this psalm. First, he acknowledges who and what the Lord is. He reminds the readers by affirming to God, ". . . thou art, holy." You see, God does not have to try and be holy by any means; He just is by what He has already done and how He always presents Himself to His people. David had the revelation of this God holy God we serve from His experiences with Him on a deeper level of worship. This exaltation of God being holy means that no wrong or filth could ever come from His being. God's purity is unmatched by His very presence, alone. Being in a relationship with a person is the only way this type of revelation can be revealed:

Relationship = *Revelation.*

Let's take a look at Matthew 16 where we will prove this statement to be true . . .

Jesus asked Peter, a fisherman who was referred to as "the rock": "Who do you say I am?"

Jesus asked this question by relationship and not by association, which he was to Peter. By mere association and without actually spending time with Christ, people mistook Him for John the Baptist, Elias, Jeremiah or just one of the prophets. Those answers show no direct connection to knowing who Jesus truly was and is. Furthermore, it was even more evident that there was no connection to the Father or to divine understanding. Those answers were born out of hearsay, from words and sights coming from the lips of those who were not connected to the Spirit. On the other hand, Peter's answers proved that not only did he spend time with the Christ, but he also spent time with the Father in spirit. He had a relationship with both the Christ and the Father.

When Peter gave his answer, he unlocked a deeper connection of trust and understanding in the realm of the spirit. There was no hesitation or unbelief in his response. Peter spoke boldly and with confidence, "Thou art the Christ, the Son of the living God (KJV)." This statement enabled Jesus to entrust Peter with greater because of the divine relationship they shared: "Blessed are you . . . for this was not revealed to you by flesh and blood, but by my Father in heaven."

A true relationship with God will unlock revelation and allow God to entrust you with His heart through His son. This relationship will release a power that is unmatched in all the earth and heaven. It permits us access to keys that will lock and unlock, to bind and to loose. The Lord will not give this type of understanding and revelation to those He does not know or trust. You will learn God's heart as you learn of His ways and mind, and as you seek His face in righteousness

David could not call the Lord holy if he did not truly know Him for himself. Now if I know the Lord and He knows me, which is key, not only do I believe and know, but I also fully trust – in the pit of my soul – that He dwells in my praise and abides in my worship. This knowing and believing confirms the relationship between God and His people, and the true connection of His people to His spirit.

If I am not saved by Jesus Christ and have not accepted Him as my Lord and Savior; He is not in my heart. How can I actually worship someone I do not serve? Do you not know that we cannot have two masters (the world and Jesus) because we will love one and hate the other? Take a moment to ask yourself, "Who am I worshipping? Why am I worshipping?" Conduct a spiritual self-check and ask the Spirit of the Lord to show you the answers to those two questions through His eyes.

It is impossible to worship anything or anyone you cannot relate to. This is key in having a relationship. In John 4, Jesus speaks of and how the Father seeketh for those to worship Him in spirit and truth. I ask, "Why is our God looking for us to worship Him?" In the book of Genesis, we interpret God missing the fellowship/relationship He shared with Adam in the cool of the day. The Lord became accustomed to spending time with Adam and it seemed as if they had lost that time. If God is seeking for us to worship Him in spirt and in truth, there must not be many of us who truly understand the mind of Christ. If God is a spirit, and He is . . . What are we?

We believe that the image and likeness we were created in, the same image and likeness the Lord spoke about in Genesis was this earthen body that must return to the dust it came from. Our true nature is that we are spirit as is our God. I will go a little further . . . the Word tells us we should know that our bodies are the temple of the Holy Spirit. Our bodies are just the temporary casing or housing for our spirits while we exist in this temporal world. I once heard a Pastor from Holland say that we are supernatural, spiritual beings having a natural, human experience while here on earth. It is almost like being on vacation for a long time until we return to our true home in glory. Ultimately, your relationship, like anything else, must begin and remain in the spirit. Just as He is Spirit, so are you. Whatever is holy, righteous, and pure must match God's Spirit.

Please note that our worship unto the Father is not a physical thing. Just because we cry, roll on the ground, shout, sing, dance or have an outward appearance of worship does not mean that what we do is actually true worship unto the Father. True worship begins in your spirit. You cannot see it, taste it, or touch it; but you can feel it in your spirit.

Your relationship with Jesus Christ must be a one–on–one relationship not based on the knowing of God, but based on truly knowing your Father Who sits in Heaven. The Lord's Prayer begins with, ". . . Our Father, which art in heaven. . ." Sometime we do not even act as if we are His children and He is our Father. In today's terminology, we act as if God, the Father, is just a baby's daddy with court-ordered visitation on our birthdays and holidays.

Our God is worth so much more and deserves much better than we are giving Him! Your spirit must connect to the Spirit (His heart), as deep calls unto deep. Jesus goes on just a little further and speaks of truth. Now, it is one thing to have a relationship with the Father, but what about a relationship with His Son? Some people just see Jesus sitting at the well of water. I see Jesus sitting by the well of water, and serving as the doorway to the entrance of living water, meaning you cannot even touch the Father without going through the Son.

The Bible declare the words of Jesus Christ, that if you have seen Him (the Son), then you have seen the Father, for they are One. We cannot kick Jesus out of His rightful place. He has paid an ultimate heavy price for our sin-filled lives and deserves to be adored, worshiped, loved, exalted, lifted up, extolled and cherished!!

If we look throughout the Bible, we see the Lord attempting to rescue Israel, His people, from worshiping statues and carnal, imaginary deities that have ears but cannot hear and lips but cannot speak – things that have no power. In doing so, God had to take His people (Israel) out of Egypt and through the wilderness, allowing supernatural things to manifest naturally to get their attention, but to also free them from themselves and their carnal worship.

The Lord has been dealing with my spirit regarding the reasons we experience problems especially when it comes to true worship and what can hinder us. A lot of the problems lie with what we intake through our spiritual gates, our eyes, and ears. Many of us have not broken away from those Egyptian mindsets and carnal ways, so our worship is carnal, fleshly and empty. These Egyptian mindsets plagued the Tribe of Israel in the Old Testament and still plague us today.

We seem to take in so much of the world (flesh) and then expect to be pure. For example, you are on the worship team or you worship in the congregation, but you still listen to and sing music that is not of God: secular music, Rap, R&B, Hip Hop, slow jams, Rock-n-Roll, etc. What you take in through your ear gates which lead to your soul (the secular music, R&B, etc.) has nothing to do with glorifying God. It is a different spirit, a familiar spirit, that edifies your flesh, not your spirit.

Have we forgotten that Satan was worship and knows everything there is to know about worship music, including how to get our flesh's attention? He knows what gets us hyped up, what gets our blood pumping, and what gets our bodies moving. He knows what hooks, beats, and musical arrangements to put together to capture our minds and flesh – the basis of our Adamic and sinful nature. His plots and schemes are wicked and "Yes; it is that serious."

We take in a lot of unacceptable, unholy spiritual junk food and expect to be true worshipers who "Arise;" but, it cannot be so. You must take in what is pure and holy to minister pure and holy worship. You can only put out what you take in. Even the Bible will tell you that a man is not defiled by what goes in, but by what comes out.

As Luke 6:45 (KJV) declares:

"A good man out of the good treasure of the heart bringeth forth that which is good; and an evil man out of the evil treasure of his heart bringeth forth that which is evil: for of the abundance of the heart his mouth speaketh."

And Matthew 6:21(KJV) informs us . . .

"For where your treasure is, there will your heart be also."

I challenge you, as you read these words, to ask yourself where your heart is.

Beyond us poisoning ourselves with this wicked spiritual food, we have no idea how the foundation of what we listen and take in to our spirit affects us. We wonder how the worldly, pythonic, antichrist spirit used to choke the life out of the anointing of God in us got into the church. Without accountability to the commandments of the Lord, we allow that spirit entry by the way we live our lives and by what we intake on a daily basis both behind closed doors and in the open.

Our ears must be continually filled with praises to the true King! Those praises should come from our spirits, but resound out of our mouths and the mouths of others. Who shall enter the hill of the Lord and who will stand in His holy place? Only those who have clean hands and a pure heart! The enemy is fighting for our attention; he is fighting for our worship. Do not give it to him!

Chapter 10

Fasting and Praying

We must have a desire to purge ourselves from the worldly things we intake, knowingly, ignorantly, or by obedience to God's spirit. This word I am about to release in this portion of the book is a word most people are going to hate, but a word I have grown to love as a child of God: Not only do we need to repent quickly, but we also need to . . . drumroll, please . . .

Get back into fasting and praying! Yes, I said it!

Now, I love to eat! Ask anyone who truly knows me and they will tell you that I will not turn down any food, especially if it's one of my favorite meals or dishes. My mother used to marvel at the amount of food I could put away with such a short stature, and others would ask in disbelief, "Boy, you still hungry?! As we continue moving through this writing, please reference the entire 58th chapter of the book of Isaiah.

As I have become more mature in the things of God, I realized that fasting and praying is not only vital to the true worshipper, but also to anyone who is truly in the kingdom of God. Most people view it as a weight loss solution. Although weight loss is one of the benefits, it should not be the reason why fasting and prayer is vital to us as the saints of God. You see, as John prayed that I must decrease so God would increase, we must do the same – pray that our flesh would die so that the spirit of the Lord would arise in us and go forth!

John the Baptist was breaking himself away from worldly cuisine to feast on heavenly manna. Fasting kills the flesh by obedience and by allowing God's spirit to maximize in your life. In short, fasting and prayer brings your spirit closer to the spirit of the Lord. In this obedient sacrifice, we allow the Lord to rid us of things that would prevent us from being closer to Him, but we also allow our spiritual ears and eyes to be sharpened concerning the things of God. Fasting and prayer also causes your spirit to come alive, to hear instruction from the Lord, and to have a greater passion for being obedient to His voice. I keep going over and over this for one reason: Obedience is better than sacrifice. The Lord is training us to hear His voice and to follow His will. You cannot be a worshipper, a follower of Jesus Christ, or a Kingdom citizen without discipline. A disciple is a disciplined solider who knows how to follow orders regardless of how he feels. True disciples want to please the one who has commissioned them. Being an air force veteran, I know the importance of this fact very well.

When I was a young Airmen going through training, the drill instructors would take us through rigorous exercises and situations to break down our will. As a result of all the things we endured, we were able to hear their voices better and to produce what was required of us. The basic training served as a fast of our will. We were molded into the will of the Air Force ways and operating procedures. Things from our lives were taken away from us so we could see how those same things would hinder us from being able to receive instruction. Our clothes, personal belongings, our time, even our food and privacy were all taken from us for the sake of conformity. Some people, unfortunately, would not consider this an example of fasting since fasting is a sacrificial choice; but I beg to differ. I made a choice to join the military of my own free will and with that choice, I signed a contract to do whatever they said, however they said it, and whenever they said it.

King Jehoshaphat, as we see in 2 Chronicles 20:3, set himself apart to receive instruction from the Lord and proclaimed a fast throughout all Judah. Because he chose to exchange an earthly need for a spiritual need, he received his answer in the spirit – Jahaziel, by the voice of the Lord, declared that the battle the king faced was not his, but God's. Without his obedient sacrifice, how was Jehoshaphat supposed to hear the voice of the Lord?

Fasting and prayer breaks our selfish will and leads us into victory! We are broken to worship!

Chapter 11

Warship/Worship

Worship is obedience and obedience is worship. Whether times are good or bad; whether there is food or no food; whether there is money or no money; whether I understand what is going on or not, whether I am sick in my body or not . . . I will worship!

David purposed in his heart, *"I will bless the Lord at all times, and His praise shall continually be in my mouth!"* Whatever was going on in his life, David's passion evoked a sweet aroma of worship and placed a smile on God's face. Worship is not for us or about what God has done for us. True worship is for Him . . . for God being God, and being God alone!

The Lord, our God is building an army of true worshipers who will worship Him in spirit and truth. I use the word "army" because we are soldiers in the Kingdom of God. The weapons of our warfare are not carnal, but mighty through God to the pulling down of strongholds. Although it is everyone's duty, not everyone is willing to be a true worshiper, broken to worship. In the book of Judges, the children of Israel were in great opposition against the Midianites, Amalekites and children of the east. No matter what they put their hands to, the enemy prevailed against them. In the sixth chapter, we learn that the children of Israel were stripped of everything and the accuser of the brethren left no sustenance for them – no sheep, no oxen no asses – and whatever they had sown was taken from them.

Even in this situation, the Lord had a plan to build His army of broken, true worshippers. He planned to bring them to the forefront so they might destroy the hands and works of the wicked one, and deliver His people. But, it takes worship. It seems like the same thing is happening in the world today with the persecution of the truth discovered with the church of Philadelphia in the book of Revelation. Like the Philadelphian church, we are to hold firmly to the things that are holy and true, and to bear the key of David which is true worship. The Lord is molding us as He did Gideon's army, but we will discover that not everyone will be able to go on this fight because they are not broken and ready.

Gideon thought it was the masses and quantity that would take the fight to the enemy and gain victory. As Gideon gathered the people unto himself, 22,000 came to fight, but the Lord said that number was too many. Man would have thought that it was by his own hand, power, and might and not by the spirit of the Lord that the victory would be won; however, the Lord reduced the number of warriors to 10,000 Israelites. Why? God's people: Just because someone proclaims to be saved doesn't mean they can go everywhere and do what God has graced you to accomplish. Still, God decided that 10,000 soldiers were still too many. I do not believe, at this moment, that Gideon understood the Lord's strategy and commandments at all, but he still fully trusted Him as a result of his "fleece experience."

The next mode of instruction was important for Gideon. You see, the Lord will always take you to the next, and the next, and the next so you are able to trust Him even more. When the Lord's instructions did not seem to line up with the situation I was facing, I learned to trust Him. He is the same God yesterday, today and always, and He will never fail me! Even when, like Gideon, you are facing three different armies whose numbers are like grasshoppers in the field and their camels are without number, God will never fail you! However, even in the midst of your battles, He is looking for quality worshippers, not the quantity of them.

The Lord instructed Gideon to take all of the men down to the water and to look for something physical, which would prove to be of great spiritual importance. As the men approached water, the Lord advised Gideon to release those who lapped up the water like dogs, having no regard for what was going on around them, and to continue on with those men who drank the water with one hand while kneeling and watching. Those were the ones God had chosen to fight. In essence, God told Gideon to take the men down to the water and watch how they worship. Those who drank the water as if they were dogs were unruly members of the body who were not yet mature in the things of God, living partially in Christ, if at all. If Gideon took them into a spiritual battle, more than likely they would have gotten both Gideon and themselves killed.

Those who cupped the water and drank it calmly, being sure to watch where the mature, broken, true worshippers were, not only were the men who worship in spirit and truth, but they were also vigilant in the realm of the spirit.

Understand the power you possess in worship! There is a "Warship" in your worship!! The word commands in Psalm 103:20 (KJV):

"Bless the Lord, ye his angels, that excel in strength, that do his commandments, hearkening unto the voice of his word."

In other words, as you worship in spirit and truth, the angels go to work on your behalf, destroying the works of the enemy. One can put a thousand to flight and two can put ten thousand to flight!! But know this: The angels cannot represent or fight for someone their boss doesn't know. You MUST have a relationship with God.

I mentioned before that this is not a natural thing, but a spiritual one. You cannot fight a spiritual battle by natural means. In these kinds of battles, you need something supernatural, something that would be foolish enough to confound the wise. Being greatly out-numbered, you would have thought the Lord would have given Gideon a strategy of arrows and steel, or even a cadre from another military regiment; but the strategy that was given was simply worship. As the trumpets blew, the power of God and the angels were dispatched to the enemies of the Lord's people. This is the only God I know who will make your enemies turn on each other while you watch! I can hear the song "Let God arise, and His enemies be scattered" ringing in my spirit!

My God, the One who sits high and looks low will only arise in your situation by worship. The Lord spoke to me one day as I was going through various tests and trials: *"When you do not know what to do and why it is happening, Worship, Watch and Wait."* When we do this and it seems like nothing is happening, know that God is behind the scenes working it all out for the good of them that love Him and are called according to His purpose!

Chapter 12

The Charge / Conclusion

I pray and charge thee woman and or man of God, that you present your bodies as living sacrifices, holy and acceptable, for this is your rightful duty to the call. I pray that you may not be conformed to this wicked world, but be transformed by the renewing of your mind, and that you walk worthy of the call that is upon your life in peace, love, favor, understanding, patience, faith and obedience. I pray that the God of the overflow will pour His spirit out onto and into willing vessels. I pray that the wisdom and revelation knowledge of who Jesus Christ is for His glory, to be manifested upon the earth and all flesh shall see it, in the mighty name of Jesus Christ be majesty, dominion, and power right now and forever more Amen!

Now be whom the Lord has called you to be and allow Him to break you to Worship!

About The Author

Pastor Jeremy J. Brown

Jeremy is a comedic-fun loving, but no non-sense follower of the Word of God through Jesus Christ being not only his Savior but Lord. He is a well-traveled 12-year Air Force Veteran and a 19-year Lieutenant in the Fire Fighting career field. Aside from that, Jeremy is also a father, pastor, prophetic worshiper, mentor and a prophetic voice crying out in the wilderness for the world to repent and be ready in these last days. In learning from his experience, not only in the world's system being lost sinful and rebellious, but also in the Kingdom of God to redemption, obedience, and salvation.

Finally, being delivered from the spirits of alcoholism, adultery, partying, smoking, generational curses and much more, it is my duty, to be led by the Holy Spirit, to be used in the same manner to live and speak truth. Going out into the world and preaching the pure, unfiltered gospel, ushering in the ministries of the prophetic, healing, deliverance and salvation until Jesus Christ return.

Jeremy is also Co-Pastor at Perfecting Faith Ministries International, under Apostle Desmond Forde located on the magnificent island of Curacao. He is the founder of the International Fresh Fire Mime and Dance Conference. He is an AA degree holder in Fire Science from the community college of the Air Force with many certifications and awards. Jeremy is from the Washington D.C area but now residing on the island of Curacao in the Caribbean with his lovely wife Leticia, son Manasseh and daughter Jaelyn who lives in the States.